CW00448140

by Iain Gray

WRITING *to* REMEMBER

79 Main Street, Newtongrange,
Midlothian EH22 4NA
Tel: 0131 344 0414   Fax: 0845 075 6085
E-mail: info@lang-syne.co.uk
www.langsyneshop.co.uk

Design by Dorothy Meikle
Printed by Printwell Ltd
© Lang Syne Publishers Ltd 2022

ISBN 978-1-85217-544-3

Roberts

MOTTO:
Go forward.

CREST:
A half lion holding a sword
(and)
An eagle.

NAME variations include:
Robart
Robarts
Robert
Robberds

Chapter one:

The origins of popular surnames

by George Forbes and Iain Gray

If you don't know where you came from, you won't know where you're going is a frequently quoted observation and one that has a particular resonance today when there has been a marked upsurge in interest in genealogy, with increasing numbers of people curious to trace their family roots.

Main sources for genealogical research include census returns and official records of births, marriages and deaths – and the key to unlocking the detail they contain is obviously a family surname, one that has been 'inherited' and passed from generation to generation.

No matter our station in life, we all have a surname – but it was not until about the middle of the fourteenth century that the practice of being identified by a particular surname became commonly established throughout the British Isles.

Previous to this, it was normal for a person to be identified through the use of only a forename.

But as population gradually increased and there were many more people with the same forename, surnames were adopted to distinguish one person, or community, from another.

Many common English surnames are patronymic in origin, meaning they stem from the forename of one's father – with 'Johnson,' for example, indicating 'son of John.'

It was the Normans, in the wake of their eleventh century conquest of Anglo-Saxon England, a pivotal moment in the nation's history, who first brought surnames into usage – although it was a gradual process.

For the Normans, these were names initially based on the title of their estates, local villages and chateaux in France to distinguish and identify these landholdings.

Such grand descriptions also helped enhance the prestige of these warlords and generally glorify their lofty positions high above the humble serfs slaving away below in the pecking order who had only single names, often with Biblical connotations as in Pierre and Jacques.

The only descriptive distinctions among the peasantry concerned their occupations, like 'Pierre the swineherd' or 'Jacques the ferryman.'

Roots of surnames that came into usage in England not only included Norman-French, but also Old French, Old Norse, Old English, Middle English, German, Latin, Greek, Hebrew and the Gaelic languages of the Celts.

The Normans themselves were originally Vikings, or 'Northmen', who raided, colonised and eventually settled down around the French coastline.

They had sailed up the Seine in their long-boats in 900AD under their ferocious leader Rollo and ruled the roost in north eastern France before sailing over to conquer England in 1066 under Duke William of Normandy – better known to posterity as William the Conqueror, or King William I of England.

Granted lands in the newly-conquered England, some of their descendants later acquired territories in Wales, Scotland and Ireland – taking not only their own surnames, but also the practice of adopting a surname, with them.

But it was in England where Norman rule and custom first impacted, particularly in relation to the adoption of surnames.

This is reflected in the famous *Domesday Book*, a massive survey of much of England and Wales, ordered by William I, to determine who owned what, what it was worth and therefore how much they were liable to pay in taxes to the voracious Royal Exchequer.

Completed in 1086 and now held in the National Archives in Kew, London, 'Domesday' was an Old English word meaning 'Day of Judgement.'

This was because, in the words of one contemporary chronicler, "its decisions, like those of the Last Judgement, are unalterable."

It had been a requirement of all those English landholders – from the richest to the poorest – that they identify themselves for the purposes of the survey and for future reference by means of a surname.

This is why the *Domesday Book*, although written in Latin as was the practice for several centuries with both civic and ecclesiastical records, is an invaluable source for the early appearance of a wide range of English surnames.

Several of these names were coined in connection with occupations.

These include Baker and Smith, while Cooks, Chamberlains, Constables and Porters were to be found carrying out duties in large medieval households.

The church's influence can be found in names such as Bishop, Friar and Monk while the popular name of Bennett derives from the late fifth to mid-sixth century Saint Benedict, founder of the Benedictine order of monks.

The early medical profession is represented by Barber, while businessmen produced names that include Merchant and Sellers.

Down at the village watermill, the names that cropped up included Millar/Miller, Walker and Fuller, while other self-explanatory trades included Cooper, Tailor, Mason and Wright.

Even the scenery was utilised as in Moor, Hill, Wood and Forrest – while the hunt and the chase supplied names that include Hunter, Falconer, Fowler and Fox.

Colours are also a source of popular surnames, as in Black, Brown, Gray/Grey, Green and White, and would have denoted the colour of the clothing the person habitually wore or, apart from the obvious exception of 'Green', one's hair colouring or even complexion.

The surname Red developed into Reid, while

Blue was rare and no-one wanted to be associated with yellow.

Rather self-important individuals took surnames that include Goodman and Wiseman, while physical attributes crept into surnames such as Small and Little.

Many families proudly boast the heraldic device known as a Coat of Arms, as featured on our front cover.

The central motif of the Coat of Arms would originally have been what was borne on the shield of a warrior to distinguish himself from others on the battlefield.

Not featured on the Coat of Arms, but highlighted on page three, is the family motto and related crest – with the latter frequently different from the central motif.

Adding further variety to the rich cultural heritage that is represented by surnames is the appearance in recent times in lists of the 100 most common names found in England of ones that include Khan, Patel and Singh – names that have proud roots in the vast sub-continent of India.

Echoes of a far distant past can still be found in our surnames and they can be borne with pride in commemoration of our forebears.

Chapter two:

Invasion and martyrdom

A surname of Anglo-Saxon roots, 'Roberts' derives from the popular forename 'Robert', meaning 'fame bright' or 'bright renown' – deriving as it does from the Germanic 'hrod', meaning 'renown' and 'beraht' indicating 'bright.'

As a surname, Roberts can mean either 'son of Robert' or 'servant of Robert', and although particularly identified with Wales it is ranked at 10th in some lists of the 100 most common surnames found in England.

Indeed it is in the English county of Kent, not Wales that the name first appears on record.

Although gaining particular popularity in the wake of the Norman Conquest of 1066, in common with many other surnames it was present in England and Wales long before this key event in history.

With its Germanic roots, this means that flowing through the veins of many bearers of the name today is the blood of those tribes who invaded and settled in the south and east of the island of Britain from about the early fifth century.

Known as the Anglo-Saxons, they were composed of the Jutes, from the area of the Jutland Peninsula in modern Denmark, the Saxons from Lower Saxony, in modern Germany and the Angles from the Angeln area of Germany.

It was the Angles who gave the name 'Engla land', or 'Aengla land' – better known as 'England.'

They held sway in what became England from approximately 550 to 1066, with the main kingdoms those of Sussex, Wessex, Northumbria, Mercia, Kent, East Anglia and Essex.

Whoever controlled the most powerful of these kingdoms was tacitly recognised as overall 'king' – one of the most noted being Alfred the Great, King of Wessex from 871 to 899.

It was during his reign that the famous *Anglo-Saxon Chronicle* was compiled – an invaluable source of Anglo-Saxon history – while Alfred was designated in early documents as *Rex Anglorum Saxonum*, King of the English Saxons. Other important Anglo-Saxon works include the epic *Beowulf* and the seventh century *Caedmon's Hymn*.

Through the Anglo-Saxons, the language known as Old English developed, later transforming from the eleventh century into Middle English –

sources from which many popular English surnames of today, such as Roberts derive.

But the death knell of Anglo-Saxon supremacy was sounded when a mighty invasion force, led by Duke William of Normandy, landed in 1066 at Hastings, in East Sussex.

The English monarch Harold II confronted them on October 14, drawing up a strong defensive at the top of Senlac Hill and building a shield wall to repel Duke William's cavalry and infantry.

The Normans suffered heavy losses, but through a combination of the deadly skill of their archers and the ferocious determination of their cavalry they eventually won the day.

Anglo-Saxon morale had collapsed on the battlefield as word spread through the ranks that Harold had been killed, and amidst the carnage of the battlefield, it was difficult to identify him – the last of the Anglo-Saxon kings.

Some sources assert William ordered his body to be thrown into the sea, while others state it was secretly buried at Waltham Abbey.

What is known with certainty, however, is that William, in celebration of his great victory, founded Battle Abbey, near the site of the battle, ordering that the altar be sited on the spot where Harold was believed to have fallen.

William was declared King of England on December 25, and the complete subjugation of his Anglo-Saxon subjects followed.

Within an astonishingly short space of time, Norman manners, customs and law were imposed on England – laying the basis for what subsequently became established 'English' custom and practice.

But beneath the surface, old Anglo-Saxon culture was not totally eradicated, with some aspects absorbed into those of the Normans, while faint echoes of the Anglo-Saxon past is still seen today in the form of popular surnames such as Roberts.

It is a name that features prominently in the frequently turbulent historical record.

Born in 1577 in the small village of Trawsfyndd in the Snowdonia area of Wales, John Roberts, later canonised as St John Roberts, was martyred for his faith during the period in English history known as 'recusancy'.

Derived from the Latin *recuso*, meaning 'I refuse', it originally applied to general acts of disobedience to the government but became mainly identified from 1549 onwards with the refusal –

particularly of Roman Catholics – to attend services of the Church of England.

Harsh penalties were meted out to recusants – including fines, forfeiture of property, imprisonment, banishment and death.

It was as a recusant that John Roberts fell victim to the most terrible of these punishments.

Baptised in to the Protestant faith and studying law, he later travelled to Europe and converted to the Catholic faith on a visit to Notre Dame Cathedral, Paris.

Becoming a member of the community of monks at St Benedict's Monastery in Valladolid, Spain and being ordained as a priest, he set off for the dangerous shores of England – dangerous, at least, for a Catholic priest – arriving there in April of 1603.

Arrested only a few weeks after his arrival after being tracked down by government spies, he was banished from the country and travelled to Douai, in northern France.

Undeterred by his previous arrest and banishment, he again clandestinely returned to England and is known to have worked tirelessly among plague victims in London from late 1603 to early 1604.

Again arrested and banished, he returned again only a short time later and in November of 1605 was arrested on suspicion of involvement in the Gunpowder Plot to blow up Parliament.

Tried and acquitted of any complicity in the abortive plot, he was nevertheless banished yet again.

Further periods of return to England and predictable banishment followed until, in December of 1610, he was arrested, tried and found guilty of ministering as a Catholic priest.

Sentenced to the horrific ordeal of being hanged, drawn and quartered he was hauled off for execution, dressed in his priest's vestments, at Tyburn on December 10.

In these particularly cruel times, it was normal practice for a man so condemned to be disembowelled while still alive.

But Roberts – because of the aid he had previously furnished to the London poor during the plague – was spared this ordeal when an angry crowd who had gathered to watch his execution persuaded the nervous authorities to allow him to be 'hanged to the death', so as not to feel the pain.

Beatified by Pope Leo XII in December of 1886, he was canonised nearly 85 years later by Pope Paul VI, on October 25, 1970, as "one of the representative Forty Martyrs of England and Wales."

Chapter three:

Honours and distinction

One particularly distinguished military family of the Roberts name can boast a father and a son who were recipients of the Victoria Cross (VC), the highest award for valour in the face of enemy action for British and Commonwealth forces.

The father and the grandfather of these respective recipients of the honour was General Sir Abraham Roberts, born in 1784 in Waterford, Ireland.

Reaching the rank of Colonel while in the service of the East India Company, he commanded the 1st Bengal European Regiment and saw action in the First Afghan War of 1838 to 1842.

This was a conflict in which Britain unsuccessfully attempted to install a puppet ruler in the face of Russian designs on the country.

It provoked a major rebellion in 1841 in Kabul and the British Army was forced into ignominious surrender – with nearly 20,000 soldiers dying in the subsequent retreat through hostile territory.

Raised to the Peerage of the United

Kingdom, by which time he had attained the rank of General, Abraham Roberts died in 1873.

He was the father of the VC recipient Field Marshall Frederick Sleigh Roberts, 1st Earl Roberts, recognised as having been one of Britain's most successful military commanders of the nineteenth century.

Born in 1832 in Cawnpore, in what was then British India, theatres of conflict in which he was involved included the Indian Mutiny of 1857 to 1858, the Second Afghan War of 1878 to 1880 and the Second Boer War of 1899 to 1902.

It was during the Indian Mutiny, in January of 1858, that he performed the actions for which he was awarded the VC.

Spotting two of the enemy who had fled a battlefield carrying aloft one of the regimental standards, he put spurs to horse and galloped off in hot pursuit.

The enemy stopped and levelled their muskets at him, but he swiftly cut them both down with his sword and restored the regiment's honour by retrieving the standard.

Later created Earl Roberts, it was following his return from the Boer War that he promoted the mass training of civilians in rifle shooting skills through shooting clubs, and this led to the creation of the National Smallbore Rifle Association.

He died in 1914, while he was the father of the posthumous VC recipient Frederick Hugh Sherston Roberts, born in 1872 in Umballa, British India.

He had been aged 27 and an officer with the King's Rifles during the Second Boer War when, in December of 1899 at the battle of Colenso, he was mortally wounded after attempting, under very heavy enemy fire, to retrieve the guns of the 14th and 66th Batteries, Royal Field Artillery.

His VC is now on display at the National Army Museum, Chelsea, while he and his father are one of only three father and son pairs to win the honour.

Another recipient of the VC, in common with Earl Roberts during the Indian Mutiny, was James Roberts, born in 1826.

He had been a private in the 9th Lancers (The Queen's Royal), when in September of 1857 at Bolundshahur he braved enemy fire to attempt to rescue a wounded comrade; he died two years later, while his VC is now displayed at the Regimental Museum of the 9th/12th Royal Lancers in Derby.

In a much different conflict and in a later century, Gordon Roberts is the former United States Army officer who was a recipient during the Vietnam War of the Medal of Honor – the nation's highest award for military valour.

Born in 1950 in Middletown, Ohio, he had been an infantryman with the 1st Battalion, 506th Infantry, 101st Airborne Division when, in July of 1969, he single-handedly destroyed three enemy machine-gun nests, saving the lives of more than 20 of his comrades.

During the Second World War, Major-General George Roberts, born in 1906 in Quetta, British India was the distinguished soldier who commanded the 11th Armoured Division, known as the "Black Bull", in North West Europe from 1944 until a year after the war's end in 1945.

In contemporary times, Andrew Roberts is the leading British historian, mainly of military warfare, born in London in 1963.

His many books include his 2008 *Master and Commanders: How Four Titans Won the War in the West* and the 2009 *The Storm of War: A New History of the Second World War*.

One particularly adventurous bearer of the

Roberts name was James Roberts, recognised as "The Father of Trekking" in Nepal.

Born in 1916 and spending his early life in India, he joined the British Indian Army in 1936 and was later posted to the 1st (King George V's Own) Ghurkha Rifles.

This allowed him to combine his army career with his passion for mountaineering, and in 1939 he scaled the 6303-metres high Himalayan peak now known as Spit Himalaya.

Further mountain ascents followed over the years and in 1964 he founded the mountaineering and trekking enterprise Mountain Travel Nepal; a recipient of the prestigious Back Award of the Royal Geographical Society, he died in 1997.

Bearers of the Roberts name have also excelled in the sciences.

Born in 1943 in Derby, Sir Richard Roberts, also known as "Rich", is the British molecular biologist and biochemist who, along with Phillip Sharp, was awarded the 1993 Nobel Prize in Physiology or Medicine for their pioneering work on the mechanism of gene-splicing.

On American shores, Anita B. Roberts, born in 1942 in Pittsburgh, Pennsylvania, was the molecular biologist who, as chief of the National Cancer Institute's laboratory of cell regulation and carcinogenesis from 1995 to 2004, made pioneering observations on a particular protein that has a role in cancers.

Elected to the American Academy of Arts and Sciences, she died in 2006.

In politics, Margaret Hilda Roberts was the British Prime Minister better known by her married name of Margaret Thatcher; this was after her marriage in 1951 to Dennis Thatcher.

The longest-serving British Prime Minister of the twentieth century and, at the time of writing, the only woman to have held the position, the frequently controversial politician was born in 1925 in Grantham, Lincolnshire, the daughter of local grocer and mayor of the town, Alfred Roberts.

Trained as a research chemist and then as a barrister, she was first elected to Parliament in 1959 as Conservative Member of Parliament (MP) for Finchley.

Defeating Edward Health for the leadership of the party in 1975 after having served in his Cabinet as Secretary of State for Education and Science, she went on to serve as British Prime Minister from 1979 to 1990.

Many of her policies, dubbed 'Thatcherism', were controversial – particularly the privatisation of state-owned companies, the drastic reduction of the power and influence of trades unions and the introduction of the highly unpopular poll tax.

Nevertheless, she does have her admirers – particularly over her decision for British forces to retake the Falkland Islands following the Argentinian invasion of 1982 – and she revelled in the nickname, coined by a Soviet journalist, of the "Iron Lady."

Resigning as Prime Minister in November of 1990 after a challenge to her leadership was launched, she retired from the House of Commons two years later and was raised to the Peerage as Baroness Thatcher.

She died in April of 2013 and received a ceremonial funeral, including full military honours and a church service at St Paul's Cathedral.

The Queen also attended the funeral – only the second time in her reign that she has attended the funeral of a former Prime Minister, the first being that of Winston Churchill in 1965.

Chapter four:

On the world stage

One of the highest paid actresses in the world, Julia Roberts was born in 1967 in Atlanta, Georgia, of a colourful mix of English, Scottish, Welsh, Irish, German and Swedish ancestry.

Abandoning childhood plans to become a veterinarian, she headed to New York after completing her high school education to pursue a career in acting.

Becoming a star in 1989 for her role in the film *Steel Magnolias*, for which she received an Academy Award nomination for Best Actress, she received a similar nomination for her role in the 1990 romantic comedy *Pretty Woman*.

Her role in the 2000 *Erin Brockovich* won her an Academy Award for Best Actress, while other box office hits in which she has starred include the 1993 *The Pelican Brief*, the 1999 *Notting Hill*, the 2003 *Mona Lisa Smile* – for which she was reputedly paid $25million – and the 2012 *Mirror Mirror*.

She is the sister of the film and television actor **Eric Roberts**, born in 1956.

Nominated for an Academy Award for Best Supporting Actor in 1985 for his role in *Runaway Train*, other big screen credits include the 1992 *Final Analysis* and the 2009 *Shannon's Rainbow*.

He is the father of the actress, model and singer **Emma Roberts**, born in 1991 in Rhinebeck, New York, and whose screen credits include the title role in the 2007 *Nancy Drew*, the 2008 *Wild Child* and the 2011 *Scream 4*.

Born in 1939 in Manhattan, New York, David Anthony Roberts is the American actor of stage and screen better known as **Tony Roberts**.

Making his Broadway debut in 1962 in the play *Something About a Soldier*, he is best known for his roles in a number of Woody Allen films that include the 1977 *Annie Hall* and the 1986 *Hannah and Her Sisters*.

Other notable film credits include the 1974 *The Taking of Pelham One Two Three* and the 2012 *The Longest Week*.

On British shores, **Ben Roberts**, born in 1950 in Bangor, Wales is the actor best known for his role of Chief Inspector Derek Conway in the television police drama *The Bill*, while big screen credits include the 2010 *Just Another Year*.

Also on British television screens, **Ivor Roberts**, born in Nottingham in 1925 and who died in 1999, was the continuity announcer and actor who played comedy roles in television series that included *Oh, Doctor Beeching*, *George and Mildred*, *Porridge* and *You Rang M'Lord?*

Behind the camera lens, **Byron Roberts** was the American film producer, assistant director and production manager whose work includes the 1957 *Baby Face Nelson*, starring Mickey Rooney and Carolyn Jones, the 1971 *The Hard Ride* and the 1976 *Logan's Run*. Born in 1910 in Brooklyn, New York, he died in 2003.

Born in London in 1899, **William Roberts** was the British screenwriter whose credits include the 1950 *The Mating Game*, the 1960 *The Magnificent Seven* and, from 1969, the Second World War film *The Bridge at Remagen*; he died in 1997.

A prolific British screenwriter and novelist, **Gareth Roberts** was born in 1968.

Best known for having written episodes of the *Doctor Who* television series and also a number of *Doctor Who* spin-off novels, he has also contributed scripts for the television soaps *Coronation Street*, *Brookside* and *Emmerdale*.

Not only an anatomist, osteoarchaeologist, paleopathologist and anthropologist but also a British television presenter, **Alice Roberts** was born in 1973 in Bristol.

Also a qualified medical doctor, the highly-talented Roberts has appeared on popular programmes that include the BBC series *Coast*, *The Incredible Human Journey*, the Channel 4 series *Time Team* and the 2012 BBC2 series *Prehistoric Autopsy*.

As an author, her books include the 2009 *The Incredible Human Journey* and the 2011 *Evolution: The Human Story*.

Bearers of the Roberts name have also excelled in the highly competitive world of sport.

On the athletics track, **Bill Roberts**, born in Salford, Lancashire in 1912 and who died in 2001, was the English sprinter who won a gold medal as a member of Britain's 4x400-metres relay team at the 1936 Olympics in Berlin.

On the rugby pitch, **Amos Roberts**, born in 1980 in Kempsey, New South Wales, is the Australian rugby league wing and fullback who, in addition to playing in Australasia's National Rugby League, also played, from 2009 to 2012, with English club Wigan Warriors.

In rugby union, **George Roberts** was the player capped five times for Scotland between 1933 and 1939.

Born in Edinburgh in 1914 and having also played for Watsonians, he was killed in action during the Second World in August of 1943 at Kanchanaburi, Thailand.

On the fields of European football, **Dave Roberts**, born in 1949, is the Welsh retired defender who, in addition to playing for teams that include Fulham, Oxford United and Cardiff City, earned 17 caps playing for the Wales national team between 1973 and 1978.

Born in 1968 in Bangor, **Iwan Roberts** is the Welsh former football striker who earned 15 caps playing for his nation in addition to playing, from 1986 to 2006, for teams that include Watford, Leicester City and Norwich City; he now pursues a career as a football commentator.

Born in 1969 in Holyhead, Wales, **Tony Roberts** is the Welsh former goalkeeper who played for his national team between 1993 and 1996 and for teams that include Queens Park Rangers, Millwall and American club Atlanta Silverbacks.

From football to the swimming pool, **David**

Evan Roberts is recognised as one of Britain's greatest-ever Paralympians.

Born in 1980 in Llantwit, Wales, it was when he was diagnosed with cerebral palsy when aged 11 that he was encouraged to take up swimming exercises as a form of physical therapy.

He has since gone on to win, at the time of writing and since 2002, an impressive haul of no fewer than eleven Paralympic gold medals in events that include the 50-metres, 100-metres and 400-metres freestyle.

Awarded an MBE for his services to disabled sport in 2005 and a CBE in 2009, he is also an inductee of the Welsh Sports Hall of Fame.

From sport to literature, **Charles Roberts** was the Canadian poet and prose writer recognised as "The Father of Canadian Poetry."

Born in 1860 in Douglas, New Brunswick, he is also known, along with Bliss Carman, Archibald Lampman and Duncan Campbell Scott, as one of Canada's school of Confederation Poets.

With his first poetry published when he was aged 18, he went on to write acclaimed works that include his 1880 *Orion and Other Poems*, the 1897 *The Book of the Native*, the 1903 *The Book of the Rose* and, from 1934, *The Iceberg and Other Poems*.

He died in 1943, while his many honours include a knighthood, election as a Fellow of the Royal Society of Canada and recognition as a Canadian Person of National Significance.

In the equally creative world of art, **David Roberts** was the Scottish painter born in 1796 in Stockbridge, Edinburgh, the son of a shoemaker.

Apprenticed for a time to a house painter and decorator, he later became a painter and designer of stage scenery before embarking on an artistic career that saw him painting not only Scottish scenes such as Melrose and Dryburgh abbeys, but also travelling to the Near East and Egypt to produce lithographic prints.

He died in 1864, while his many works include his 1840 *A View in Cairo*, the 1850 *The Destruction of Jerusalem* and, from 1858, *Edinburgh from the Calton Hill*.

In contemporary music, **Brad Roberts**, born in 1964 in Winnipeg and his brother **Dan Roberts**, born in 1967, are founding members of the Canadian folk-rock band Crash Test Dummies.

Internationally best-selling albums they have

recorded include the 1991 *The Ghosts That Haunt Me*, the 2001 *I Don't Care That You Don't Mind* and the 2004 *Songs of the Unforgiven*.

Born in 1946 in Harrow, Middlesex, **Andy Roberts** is the English singer, songwriter, guitarist and professionally trained violinist who has played for artistes and bands that include Roy Harper, Pink Floyd and Kevin Ayers.

Born in 1936 in Greenville, South Carolina, **Billy Roberts** is the American musician and songwriter best known for having written the rock song *Hey Joe* – a major hit for The Jimi Hendrix Experience.

Bearers of the proud name of Roberts have also proven to have had a particular aptitude for invention.

Born in Chester in 1859, **David Roberts** is recognised as the inventor of the caterpillar track – used to this day on tanks and other military vehicles in addition to heavy trucks used in construction.

It was in 1903 that the British War Office offered a £1000 prize for a tractor that could haul a load of 25 tons for 40 miles without having to stop for fuel or water.

A trained hydraulic engineer and working as

chief engineer for Richard Hornsby and Sons, Roberts not only successfully rose to the challenge but also made the tractor capable of traversing water-logged and muddy surfaces.

This was through the use of what became known as caterpillar tracks, used on British tanks deployed on the Western Front during the First World War; the inventor died in 1928.

In contemporary times, Henry Edward Roberts, born in 1941 in Miami, Florida and better known as **Ed Roberts**, was the American engineer and entrepreneur known as "The Father of the Personal Computer."

It was in 1975 that he invented the first commercially successful personal computer after having five years earlier founded Micro Instrumentation and Telemetry Systems (MITS); he died in 2010.